"Life is not measured by the number of breaths you take but by the moments that take your breath away."
~Maya Angelo

Foreword

I have known the author for more than a quarter of a century after first meeting him at the University of North Texas in Denton. During his undergraduate days, Steven Dean Loewenstein's incredible talent for capturing the essence of the Reverend Dr. Martin Luther King, Jr. was nothing short of amazing! Never in my more than thirty years in higher education administration, had I heard or seen anyone quite like Steven Dean Loewenstein express the "who, what and why" while delivering the profound messages of Dr. King. His facial expressions, hand gestures, pronunciation, and tonality capture his audience as they travel with Dr. King through America's historic journey of segregation and civil rights. I have seen Steven Dean present Dr. King's messages to more than a dozen audiences from Texas to California, and his commitment and dedication to social justice is a heartfelt passion that only seems to increase over time.

Here we are today, several decades later, when our nation so desperately needs to reconnect with itself. It's no surprise that Steven Dean stepped forward to answer the call with his book, *A President, A King and You*, a poignant social and racial justice action plan for unifying readers. *A President, A King and You* aims for the collective good of keeping us together through rhythmic and artistic visioning, and engaging young readers as part of the harmonic solution.

A President, A King and You is a wonderfully creative and artistically illustrated book that highlights the life, works, and hearts of two of America's greatest leaders and heroes – President Abraham Lincoln and the Reverend Dr. Martin Luther King, Jr. It engages *you* from the very beginning by including YOU in the title, the story, and the solution! From the catchy lyrics and rhythmic rap to the beautifully illustrated characters, Mr. Loewenstein immerses YOU, the reader, in an honest but fun way of learning about some of our country's darkest days.

Steven Dean Loewenstein's talent abounds, but his love for education and teaching future generations is clearly his heart! Each character in the book, outside of President Lincoln and Dr. King, represents individuals who have played a major role in his life. With each page, you will realize that YOU cannot just read *A President, A King and You*. YOU will find that to read the book is to experience this powerful story with your eyes, your ears, and most importantly with your heart. As YOU will soon see, this is not just a book . . . it's a message. Allow it to take your breath away!

        Wm. Gregory Sawyer, Ph.D.
        Founding Vice President for Student Affairs
        California State University Channel Island
        and former Founding Dean of Student Services at Florida Gulf Coast University
        and Dean of Students at University of North Texas

Mr. And Mrs. Sergeant Major Phillips. Mr. Phillips is a Purple Heart recipient and a veteran of the Korean and Vietnam Wars.

LOVE

From left to right: Mrs. Phillips, the author, and his Aunt Malinda Marlin, former principal of LeBarron Elementary, at church in El Paso, TX.

DREAM BIG

The author and his best friend, Chris, who are the inspiration for Kool Aid and Professor C.K.P.

BROTHERHOOD

Dedication

I dedicate this book to my family next door growing up as a child, the Phillips. Mr. and Mrs. Sergeant Major Phillips and their youngest son, Chris, are an African American family from Alabama who settled in the city of El Paso. Chris and I grew up as brothers, hoopsters, and best friends in the seventies and eighties. We, as many of you, are fruit of Dr. King's dream.

Big thanks to my illustrator, Megan Regenold for being such a pleasure and joy to work with during the entire process. A very heartfelt thanks to the small but very special group of people who also helped bring my dream into reality: Dr. Wm. Gregory Sawyer, Ph.D, Dr. Rita Sawyer, Ph.D, Lyndi and Collin Jones, Marcus Jones, Kellie Vaughan, Monica Lozano Hughes, Caroline Carter, Karsten Hatcher, Bonnie Belknap, Tina Taylor, Erin Staniszewski, Lilyan Prado, Donald Cox, Pastor Timothy and First Lady Arzetta Henderson, Natalie Kirchoff, Coach Mike Morrison, my daughter Leigh, aka: Sprinkles, and my wife, Melanie Loewenstein, Ph.D. Reading Education.

I dedicate this book to President Lincoln, to Dr. King, and to the other heroes named on the pages of this book. But not only that, I dedicate this book to the countless and courageous people whose names we may never know, but who lived through the long night of slavery and segregation, while hoping for and believing in a brighter day for their children, descendants, and country.

Finally, and most importantly, I dedicate this book to YOU, to children and to young people everywhere. Listen to your parents, coaches and teachers. Believe, work hard and know this... YOUR DREAMS will continue to inspire and change the world!

-Steven D. Loewenstein

The service dog depicted in this book is based off the author's own dog, Golden.

JOY

DREAM NOW

The author's daughter, Leigh, set the state record in the 50 yard freestyle, 9-10 year old girls' division, while she was in 5th grade at the 2014 TAAF State Championships.

FAITH

A President, A King, And YOU!

Written by Steven D. Loewenstein
Illustrations by Megan E. Regenold

Please visit www.apakayou.com for a free fully rendered musical version of the book to read or sing along to as well as other educational resources!

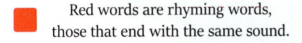 Red words are rhyming words, those that end with the same sound.

 Striped words are stressed words, those that do not end in exactly the same sound but share a similar sound, such as a long vowel.

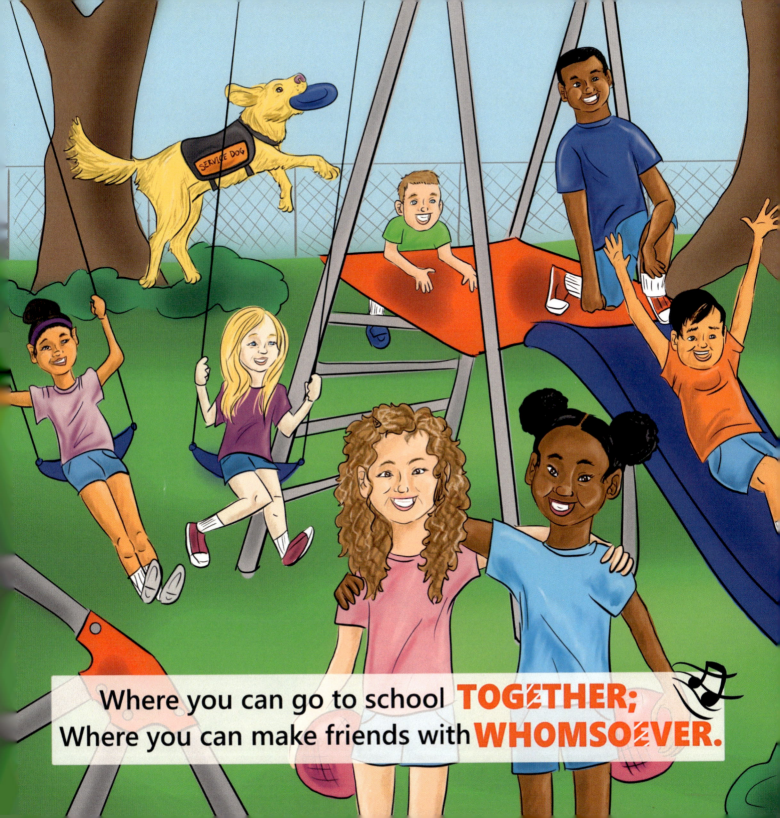

A slave was someone who was forced to work for free his or her entire life. A slave was viewed as property to be owned, not a person to be respected.

Your skin color or **SHADE,**
Decided if you were born free or a **SLAVE.**

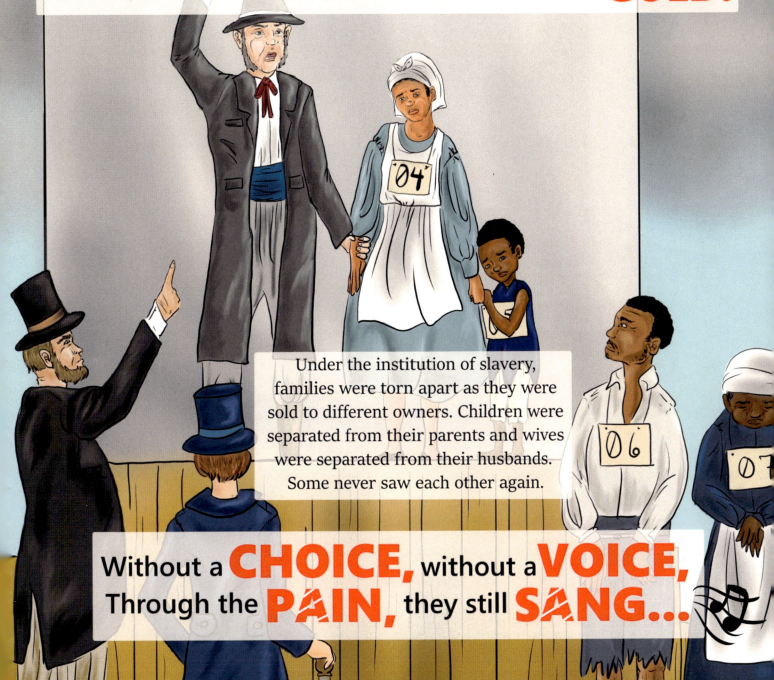

But these evil **WAYS,** Lasted over 90,000 **DAYS.**

The system of slavery lasted over 245 years on U.S. soil.

1619--**1865**

1619
First slaves landed
in Jamestown, VA

1865
Slavery officially abolished
with the passing of the 13th Amendment

DOM RING

"Let freedom ring from the snow capped Rockies of Colorado!" proclaimed Dr. King, in his famous "I Have A Dream" speech. He gave this speech on the steps of the Lincoln Memorial in Washington D.C. on August 28, 1963, one hundred years after President Abraham Lincoln signed the Emancipation Proclamation. When Dr. King declared "let freedom ring," he was referencing the lyrics within the American patriotic song, "My Country Tis of Thee," written by Samuel Francis Smith.

Segregated busing became a thing of the PAST, The Supreme Court ruled it wouldn't LAST!

On November 13, 1956 the Supreme Court ruled that segregated busing was unconstitutional.

So they marched, prayed, and SANG...

Dr. King and friend, Ralph Abernathy, kneel in prayer on "Turnaround Tuesday," March 9, 1965.

There were three attempts to march from Selma to Montgomery for voting rights. The first was March 7, "Bloody Sunday." The second was March 9, known as "Turnaround Tuesday," as they prayed and then turned back in fear of more bloodshed. The third attempt was successful. President Johnson federalized the National Guard and over 3,000 people began the 54 mile march down Highway 80 on March 21. Five days later, the march had grown to 25,000 people and culminated on the steps of the capitol building in Montgomery, Alabama. It is here, on March 25, 1965, that Dr. King delivered his compelling speech, "How Long, Not Long."

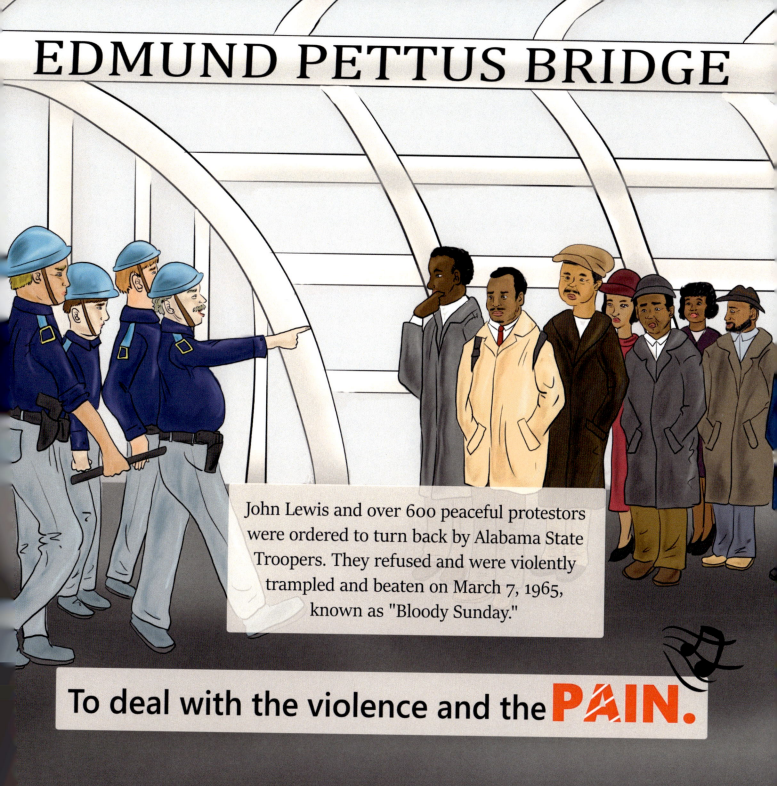

Will you be a DOCTOR, a LAWYER, or a TEACHER?

Orlando K. Beckum, MD states that "Biology is chemistry, chemistry is physics, physics is math, and math is everything." For a full explanation of this quote, visit www.apakayou.com

Catherine Cortez Masto, lawyer and the first Latina Senator in the United States.

Coach Steven Loewenstein, Physical Education teacher, motivational speaker, and author.

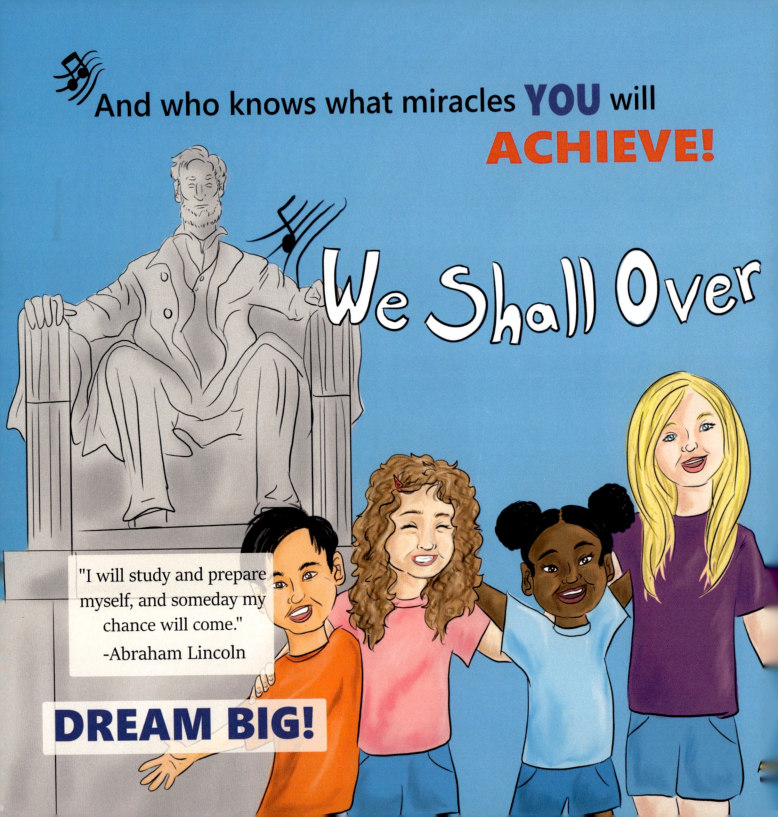

Glossary of Historical People (In Order of Appearance)

President Abraham Lincoln (February 12, 1809-April 11, 1865) an American statesman and lawyer who served as the 16th President of the United States from March of 1861 until his assassination in April of 1865.

Dr. Martin Luther King Jr. (January 15, 1929-April 4, 1968) an American Baptist preacher who led the Civil Rights Movement by the method of non-violent peaceful protest and love. Dr. King was not a medical doctor but a doctor of philosophy (Ph.D.). A Ph.D. is the highest academic degree awarded and requires at least 4 years of study, extensive research, and a Bachelor's degree. Martin graduated from high school at age 15. He earned his Bachelor's of Arts degree in Sociology from Morehouse College, his Bachelor's of Divinity from Crozer Theological Seminary and his Ph.D. from Boston University in 1955.

Rosa Parks (February 4, 1913-October 24, 2005) an African American activist, author, and known as the "Mother of the Civil Rights Movement" for refusing to give her seat to a white person on a city bus in Montgomery, Alabama in 1955. Rosa was arrested, which led to the Montgomery Bus Boycott and the Supreme Court decision to desegregate public transportation on November 13, 1956.

Carl Matthews (circa 1932-February 26, 2016) the Winston-Salem, North Carolina sit-in leader. On February 8, 1960 he sat at a Kress store to protest segregated lunch counters. 107 days later on May 25, 1960 after a desegregation agreement was signed he became the first African American person to be served at a desegregated open lunch counter.

Bill Stevens a white student at Wake Forest University in Winston-Salem, NC who sat in with Carl Mathews in protest of segregated lunch counters.

Margaret Ann Dutton a white student at Wake Forest University in Winston-Salem, NC who also sat in with Carl Mathews in protest of segregated lunch counters.

Mother Pollard (circa 1882-1885 to circa 1963) an African American woman who lived in Montgomery, Alabama. She was a great source of inspiration to Dr. King during the Montgomery Bus Boycott encouraging Martin, "I done told you we is with you, all the way but even if we ain't with you, God's gonna take care of you!" She is also known for participating in the Montgomery Bus Boycott at an advanced age.

Ruby Bridges (September 8, 1954-) the first African American child to desegregate an all white school, William Frantz Elementary in New Orleans, Louisiana on November 14th, 1960.

Glossary of Historical People (In Order of Appearance)

Ralph Abernathy (March 11, 1926-April 17, 1990) a Baptist minister, civil rights leader and close friend of Dr. Martin Luther King Jr.

John Lewis (February 21, 1940-) a congressman serving Georgia's 5th Congressional district since 1987. He served as chairman of the Student Nonviolent Coordinating Committee (SNCC). He helped lead the marches from Selma to Montgomery. Congressman Lewis is recognized as one of the most important leaders of the Civil Rights Movement.

Abraham Heschel (January 11, 1907-December 23, 1972) a Polish born American Rabbi. He marched and stood with Dr. King during the Civil Rights Movement.

Coretta Scott King (April 27, 1927-January 30, 2006) an American author, civil rights activist and the wife of Dr. Martin Luther King Jr.

Jesse Jackson (October 8, 1941-) an American civil rights activist, Baptist minister and politician. He was a key contributor to the Civil Rights Movement and part of Dr. King's inner circle.

President Lyndon B. Johnson (August 27 1908-January 22, 1973), often referred to as LBJ, was the 36th president of the United States, and was instrumental in getting the Civil Rights Act of 1964 and the Voting Rights Act of 1965 passed.

Orlando K. Beckum, MD (January 28 1972-) a medical doctor who lives and works in the Houston area. He and the author attended college together at the University of North Texas and are the best of friends.

President Barack Obama (August 4, 1961-) the 44th President of the United States of America and the first African American to hold the office of the presidency. Obama's slogan while on the campaign trail was, "Yes we can!" He served two terms as President from 2009 to 2017.

Bernice King (March 28, 1963-) an American minister and the daughter and youngest child of Dr. Martin Luther King Jr.

Catherine Cortez Masto (March 29, 1964-) an American lawyer. In 2016, she became the first Latina woman to be elected to the United States Senate. She represents the state of Nevada.

Vocabulary and Historical Terms (In Alphabetical Order)

Civil Rights are rights given to all American citizens by the Constitution of the United States and other acts of Congress. Especially the rights of personal liberty guaranteed by the thirteenth and fourteenth amendments. They are meant to ensure political freedom, social freedom, and equality.

Civil Rights Act of 1964 a landmark law that ended legal segregation in public places and banned employment discrimination on the basis of race, color, religion, sex or national origin. It was signed by President Johnson on July 2, 1964.

Civil Rights Movement a struggle by African Americans aided by empathetic white people and people from varying racial and cultural backgrounds in the mid 1950's to late 1960's to achieve **Civil Rights.** Those rights included equal opportunity in employment, housing and education. They also included access to the use of public facilities such as restrooms, swimming pools and parks.

Constitution of the United States a document that embodies the fundamental laws and principles by which the United States is governed. It was drafted by the Constitutional Convention and later supplemented by the Bill of Rights and other amendments. James Madison is credited with writing the document that formed the model for the Constitution. It was signed September 17, 1787. The first lines of the Constitution are, "We the people of the United States, in order to form a more perfect union..."

Declaration of Independence a document declaring the thirteen American Colonies independent from Great Britain. It was written by Thomas Jefferson and declared in effect by the Continental Congress on July 4, 1776. The first lines of the Declaration of Independence are, "When in the course of human events..."

Emancipation Proclamation a presidential proclamation and executive order signed by President Abraham Lincoln on January 1, 1863. It states "that all persons held as slaves within the rebellious states are, and henceforward shall be forever free." The freedom, promised by the declaration, was dependent on Union military victory because it only applied to states that had seceded from the Union or had not already come under Northern control. The proclamation allowed African Americans to join the Union Army which helped the North win the war over the South and eventually led to the passing of the 13th amendment which abolished slavery permanently.

Integration a system intended to remove barriers to equal opportunity so that people of different races, cultures, religions and creeds can enjoy the same civil rights.

Montgomery Bus Boycott a political and social protest against the policy of racial segregation on the public transit system in Montgomery, Alabama. It started on December 5, 1955 and ended on December 20, 1956 after the Supreme Court ruled against segregated busing.

Racism prejudice or discrimination directed against someone of a different race based on the belief that one's own race is superior.

Segregation a system of laws that took root after slavery ended, which severely limited the rights of African Americans and separated them from white people in all aspects of life.

Service Dog a dog trained to do work or perform tasks for the benefit of an individual with a disability, be it physical, mental, or sensory related.

Slavery the forced servitude of one person or people by another person or people.

Spent an adjective meaning exhausted, be it physically, mentally, or emotionally. Mrs. Rosa Parks was emotionally tired of the system of segregation and refused to give her seat to a white man boarding the bus she rode on December 1, 1955. *She stayed in her seat because she was **spent**.*

Supreme Court the highest federal court in the United States. It takes judicial precedence over all other courts in our nation. It is made up of nine justices and is located in Washington, D.C.

Thirteenth Amendment an amendment to the United States Constitution that abolished slavery and involuntary servitude. It was ratified by Congress on December 6, 1865.

Voting Rights Act of 1965 a law signed by President Johnson on August 6, 1965. It outlawed discriminatory voting practices put into place after the Civil War, including literacy tests and poll taxes. It is considered by many the crowning achievement of the Civil Rights Movement.

Whomsoever a pronoun, used instead of *whosoever* as the object of a verb or preposition.

About the Author Steven D. Loewenstein is a husband and the father of one beautiful and talented daughter. He is a physical education teacher, swim coach and author. He has had his own academic, social and family challenges to overcome. He is mildly autistic, an adult child of alcoholic parents, and has experienced the pain of his own biological parents' divorce as a child.

Dr. King's speeches and sermons became a great source of inspiration to him growing up. Dr. King's words continued to inspire him as a college student. Since then, he has performed reenactments of Dr. King's most beloved sermons and speeches with diverse audiences.

In 2011, he was invited to the dedication of the Martin Luther King Jr. Memorial in Washington, D.C., where he performed Dr. King's powerful sermon, "The Drum Major Instinct." Much earlier in his career in 1996, he was blessed with the opportunity to meet, hug, and perform for Mrs. Rosa Parks. After the program, he fondly remembers her kind comment to him, "You did such a good job!"

To contact Steven in regards to him sharing a Dr. King reenactment for your group go to:
www.montgomerytomemphis.com

To contact Steven in regards to sharing his book with your school, students, or group go to:
www.apakayou.com
Presentations include a reading and rapping of the book as well as a Dream Big and Now goal setting session.

About the Illustrator Megan Regenold is a wife, daughter, aunt, and artist. She lives in Texas with her husband and cat, and draws from time to time. She graduated with a Bachelor's of Arts in History from the University of North Texas. You can follow her work at the facebook page "Megaregen Creations."

For a free musical version of the book, educational resources, printable goal charts, and much more, visit:

www.apakayou.com

A President, A King, and

_____

(Write your name here!)